Old East Kilbride

by

Stuart Marshall

The Wee Toll — The most photographed location of Edwardian East Kilbride, seen here circa 1907 with a post boy standing outside. The Wee Toll is now occupied by E.K. Copyprint.

First published in the United Kingdom, 1994,
by Stenlake Publishing Ltd.
Telephone: 01290 551122
www.stenlake.co.uk
ISBN 9781872074436

Every town and village had a 'lovers lane' and East Kilbride was no exception. But the council and the development corporation built houses over the spot — practical but unromantic! Never mind, there wasn't much chance of a quiet canoodle with that crowd around anyway!

Despite its other charms, East Kilbride is perhaps best known for its roundabouts, a sufficient novelty in 1961 to be the subject of picture postcards. This is, of course, the Whitemoss Roundabout, situated near to the Territorial Army's HQ and St. Bride's Church, or as locals call it — "Fort Apache".

Montgomery Street circa 1909. This is still a recognisable view although the two buildings visible on Kittoch Street have gone. Montgomery Street is currently 'on the up' — boutiques and other smart shops have replaced the traditional village traders.

One commercial survivor on Mongomery Street is the chip shop — a haunt of mine on Saturday nights of old — after being chucked out of the 'Monty' at lousing time. Now very smart, if a bit twee, the street is much changed since this 1921 view.

The 'Monty' dates from 1719 and even when this postcard was published round about 1913, was in use as a traditional coaching inn. Bucking the general trend, the 'Monty' has 'lost' its dormer windows. The Loupin on Stane, here being demonstrated by a young lad, was to help the customer mount (or fall onto?) his horse.

At the time of writing, it's only a few weeks since a friend of mine, someone who's lived in the town for all their forty odd years, and has drunk in the 'Monty' regularly, noticed the Loupin on Stane for the first time!

A birds eye view from the church steeple looking east down Glebe Street circa 1910.

East Kilbride had a Post Office from 1833–34. It was initially located at the corner of Glebe and Hunter Streets. At some point it moved down Glebe Street to number 19, seen above. Although the postcard is Edwardian, it was clearly not the 'old' Post Office when the photograph was taken and so probably dates from the mid 1890s.

In 1898 the Post Office was on the move again, this time to 7 Montgomery Street, the building to the right of this circa 1905 picture.

And the Post Office had itchy feet once more when it moved to this now demolished building in Maxwell Road (then Maxwelton Road) in 1913. This time before the First World War was the golden age of the postal service and the picture postcard. Over half a billion postcards sent through the UK mail each year and five deliveries a day, even in rural areas, kept the Post Office busy!

Kate Dalrymple's House stood at the corner of Maxwell Street and Main Street opposite the Cross Roads Inn. But who was she? Kate Dalrymple was a once-famous song set to the tune of 'Jinglin Johnnie' by a long forgotten local poet William Watt. She is said to have been a character conjured from Watt's mind and her association with the cottage became a local legend born of misunderstanding. Whatever the truth, following the local tradition of not letting sentiment interfere with progress, the cottage was obliterated in the early 1930s to be replaced by a bank building.

As the old village is tarted up, it must be with some regret that the powers that be look at pictures of what was lost not so long ago. Maxwell Street, seen above around 1910, has suffered badly.

The bowling club was established in 1872 and is seen here in Edwardian times. Bowling has, perhaps surprisingly, become a very big sport in East Kilbride — the younger element being actively encouraged.

The Threshold Brae, Maxwell Road, 1913. Here now, on the right, can be found the 'Threshold Assembly Hall' and 'Kirkpatrick Substation'. This postcard's message reads 'Up this road on the right is an avenue leading to White Moss. Mr Sweenie is a great pansy grower, knows Smillie of Busby of whom he speaks well.'

The village smithy was located at the corner of Hunter and Montgomery Streets, adjacent to the Montgomery Inn, where the box-shaped benches are now. With the passing of coaching times the smithy's days were inevitably numbered.

The message on the back of this Edwardian postcard reads: "Dear Brother we are very disappointed at you not coming on Saturday we think you could bring Maggie and Jeannie with you if not could you not let Maggie or Jeannie come with Mary on Friday James as run ashore he must see is father on Saturday yours truly John Broomhall what a glorious day Grandfather had on Tuesday."

Main Street, 1904 looking in the direction of the Torrance Hotel.

Main Street circa 1911, again virtually unrecognisable. Robert Jope was one of East Kilbride's native postcard publishers — where better to photograph than your own shop?

Next stop for Robert Jope was the public school seen here in 1911. It later became a Secondary Modern. It is now an annexe to Cambuslang College.

Opposite the school portals and adjacent to the Torrance Hotel was a small brewery. 19Th century life in the village was awash with sleaze. Around 1840 a total of 19 pubs and inns served a parish population of about 3,600, much to the dismay of the minister, while earlier that century the village had four brothels 'serving' a population of about 500! The bad old good old days!

Torrance Square circa 1910. The square had two previous names — Stuarton and Cotton Square, so named after General Stuart of Torrance who built the cotton mill in 1783. In 1792, the works moved to Newhouse Mill and part of the building became an inn to serve traffic on the newly opened turnpike road to Glasgow. In 1885 the Inn was renamed the Torrance Hotel.

Torrance Square in the mid 1950s. Visible are the Parish Council Chambers (1913) and the Old Men's Rest, which I can personally vouch from my courting days, was used not just by old men! Sadly, the "rest" has now been replaced by a toilet block.

Looking towards the town from Market Hill, circa 1928. The picture has been taken from about the present-day junction with Dalrymple Drive, but it's hard to tell as the area is so built up now. Market Hill takes its name from when temporary markets were held here with Glasgow traders so as to keep the danger of plague at a safe distance from the village.

Young girls play on a long 1904's summer day on the White Moss Road.

Outside Leigh Markethill Cottage (now an office supplies shop) sits an effigy of Sir Walter Scott. According to the story, the sculptor was so unhappy with his work that the sculpture was buried, only to be "disinterred" some time later. He continues to have a hard life — he's weather worn and over painted — and his head and nose have been knocked off many times. However, he has acquired half a left foot since this Edwardian postcard photo was taken!

Parkhall Street was the town's main street until the Glasgow to Strathaven turnpike road was built in the 1790s. It was then relegated to becoming 'Back Row'. Although the presence of Montgomery Street in the background gives a clue to the locus of the scene, the buildings in the foreground are gone and the road has been re-aligned.

'The X shows the house we are living in' writes the proud correspondent on this 1930s view of a (very quiet) Kirktonholme Road. Two houses have since been built on the gap site on the right. It's so much busier today!

The playground in the public park, circa 1912. There is still a play park here, also used by East Kilbride Thistle. Some people say that they play here, others, unkindly, say that "it's just eleven East Kilbride players standing on a park". In 1983 they beat Bo'ness United 2–0 at Hampden to win the Scottish Junior Cup — and they've been getting worse ever since! In 1994 they were relegated from the Premier Division of the Reebok League after a season of being the strongest team — for propping the rest of the league up!

Edwardian East Kilbride was a popular holiday destination and 'tourism' contributed strongly to the local economy. Today, the tourist board entices the summer visitors with the shopping and leisure facilities. Back then fresh air and the numerous country walks in the unspoilt surrounding countryside were the attractions.

Lymkilns house. This used to stand on a site opposite the Kirktonholme playing fields. Seen above in its heyday, it was later used as a cattery before succumbing to demolition. It's all built over now.

'Cairns became Reid' is pencilled on the back of this 1910 photograph, a clue to the identity of one or more of the men working the steam digger in what is probably one of the many limestone quarries that at one time operated in the parish. Limestone quarrying and burning was a major source of local employment from the mid 18th to early 20th centuries.

1906 with the railway as the necessary landmark, as this view is radically different now. On the left is Kirktonholme Road and just visible on the right, The Wee Toll. Ironically, this was how it looked before all the overspill housing from the "dear green place" was built.

But the interior of the railway station looks much the same today as it did in this 1906 photo. The railway reached East Kilbride in 1868 and provided the impetus to developing East Kilbride as a "health resort".

The writer of this card tells us "We had a run down here yesterday to a Sunday School picnic. "Lovely place two stations past Giffnock" Today, Thornton Hall is the haunt of the seriously rich. The 'normal' trains stop here on their way to East Kilbride, but "The Bullet" and other so-called express trains don't. And most of the time they still don't manage to reach East Kilbride on time.

In this comic card, the visitors seem eager to leave, a sentiment shared by one postcard writer whose message reads "Wish I was at Ardrossan. This is so quiet"

The message on this 1905 postcard on Long Calderwood Farm explains "The middle cottage is the birthplace of the famous physicians Drs William and John Hunter. In 1762 the former was appointed physician extraordinary to the Queen and in 1768 he was elected Professor of Anatomy in the Royal Academy. He formed one of the most splendid anatomical museums in the world. It eventually found its way to the University of Glasgow and formed the basis for the Hunterian Museum. Edward Jenner the discoverer of vaccination was a pupil of Dr John Lister". Another correspondent was less enthralled. "This is where a famous doctor was born, but we forget his name".

Cantislaw Farm is one of the "lost farms" and was situated next to Maxwellton, where Cantislaw Drive is now.

Maxwellton was at one time a separate village, said to have come into existence around 1780 and the domain of hand loom weavers. Another name for it was the self-explanatory "Hogsmuir". Although the surrounding area has been built up, the village remains remarkably intact with only piecemeal demolition and replacement.

Posted in August 1911, this postcard view taken further up the street was sent by George Gow of 8 Maxwellton to a Mrs Cameron of Strachur. "Our house is marked with an X and my oldest boy is opposite with white suit against the wall. Harry Alfred Long Gow".

This 1930 postcard was sent by one of the tiny visitors Archie on his fresh air fortnight, back to his "mammy", Mrs Dyke of Mill Street, Rutherglen — a poor area of decrepit tenements that have now all been swept away. He tells her he is "keeping all right" and "how we got our photos taken on Monday". At the beginning of the Second World War, the home was commandeered by the military and from 1940 it was used as a home for maladjusted and disturbed evacuee children. In 1941 it narrowly missed taking a direct hit in a bombing raid and today is Nerston School.

Stoneymeadow lay on the old Hamilton Road and the little shop seen here was at one time a toll house on the turnpike road. These cottages are no more.

Calderwood Castle was an ancient seat, much extended in the middle of the 19th century by the baronet of Calderwood. In 1904 the castle and its beautiful estate were bought by the Scottish Co-operative Wholesale society to use for fruit growing and the estate subsequently became a popular visitor attraction. The Caledonian Railway even issued a set of postcards to advertise its charms and built a platform to serve the visitors to the estate.

The Poet Tannahil waxed lyrical about Calderwood Glen in one of his songs, but the glen's charm and natural beauty were enhanced by these man made attractions which lay down river from the waterfall.

During the First World War, the castle was occupied by Belgian refugees. In 1935, the SCWS sold the estate and the castle, no long maintained, fell into disrepair. Here it is seen after the war prior to the final stages of demolition. The steps in the foreground of the picture on page forty two and odd bits of stone are all that now remain.

The Calderwood Estate, together with the Torrance Estate, now together constitute the Calderglen Country Park. The main entrance to the park is at the lodge picture above.

Crutherland House was another of the local big houses, but it is now a hotel. I can personally recommend it for that intimate meal.

Left: The joys of being on holiday?
Right: Mains castle was built in 1450 by the Lindsays of Dunrod, but was abandoned in 1670. After being roofless for nearly 300 years, it was bought by Mike Rowan for £500 in 1976. Much restoration work later, it is now used for corporate entertaining in the "traditional Scottish manner". Between playing laird and host, Mike tours the world as "Big Rory" — the giant, kilted piper on stilts!

Fair Monday, 1920. Cycle out here from Strathaven — between 7 or 8 miles. Have just finished our lunch and are now engaged in admiring the scenery which consists of view you see on the other side and in killing flies. Cousin Isabella Mackie" Sent to Master McGregor, The Mill, Motherwell.

Messages on the backs of postcards from Jackton extol its praises. "The air and the country is lovely here" is typical of such remarks. During World War Two, the village had a different type of visitor, children evacuated from Glasgow and the Clydebank Blitz. I used to go cross-country running with the school to here, from Duncanrig to Jackton where I'd have a rest on the park swings, then back over Gardenhall and Mossneuk, where the houses are now.

Stuart Street in the early 1960s. Is that a Rover P4 and an Austin A30 on the right?

Kirkton Park circa 1960, but very similar today.

There's another A40 and a Central SMT Leyland Chieftan bus in this 1963/63 photo of Churchill Avenue. All the main bus stops were here until the early 1980s. Sent in 1963, Bett's message captures the spirit of the age: "Having a quiet time but miss might night out at the club, also bingo However I feel better and there is a big change up here Houses and shops everywhere".

Murray Square in the early 1960s, in the golden age of British motoring, when cars looked like cars and not the jelly moulds of today. Visible in this picture are, amongst other vehicles, a Lyons Tea Commer Van, an Austin A35, an early Mini, a Lambretta Scooter and, in the foreground, a Bond minicar, made in Preston — no reverse gear and a top speed of 45 m.p.h.

This is what the Town Centre was like when I arrived in East Kilbride in 1963. In the car park are a Riley Pathfinder, Bedford CA Van, Morris Minor and the obligatory Austin A35. Only buses are allowed in here now.

My most unusual postcard find! It was only like this for a short time. Another early 1960s view of the Town Centre, but can you work out where this is?

Already gone from the "new" East Kilbride is the famous fountain. People threw coins into it, as people do, and children fell or were pushed in! As a result it was filled up, and became a flower bed, but was vandalised and finally the "fountain" was removed altogether.